# the HONEYMOONERS

Annie McGarry

MALLARD PRESS

Copyright © 1992 by Brompton Books
Corporation

First published in the United States of America in
1992 by The Mallard Press
Mallard Press and its accompanying design and
logo are trademarks of BDD Promotional Book
Company, Inc.

ISBN 0-7924-5546-0

Printed in Hong Kong

Designed by Tom Debolski

# CONTENTS

# AND AWAY WE GO

**J**ackie Gleason, creator, writer, director and star of **The Honeymooners**, is the man credited with selling many American families their first television. It is said that on a warm Saturday night when people had their windows open, you could hear the entire program by walking down any street in America. It was coming out of every house.

The police noticed that there was less traffic than usual, and theatre managers reported a decline in business. Estimates of Jackie's viewership after his first year on CBS are around 60 million.

Before he had a stage, John Herbert Gleason had the neighborhood in the Bushwick section of Brooklyn. Jackie'd be hanging out in front of Freitag the Delicatessan's (sic), busting the chops of the passers-by, swinging his keychain, looking natty and being a wisenheimer (a bit of Brooklynese that Jackie brought to the rest of the world). His sense of humor showed itself early. At age two, he temporarily relieved the melancholy of the mourners at his brother's funeral when he was discovered putting rubberbands around the legs of the horses pulling the hearse. He explained that they were garters to hold up the horses' white socks.

In school, he was known for making jokes at the principal's expense. At his grade school graduation, he delivered a hilarious rendition of 'Little Red Riding Hood' in a Yiddish dialect. He spent much of his youth hanging out with the Nomads, his neighborhood 'club,' shooting baskets at PS 73. Finally, he found a stage at the Halsey Theatre on amateur nights, where he could be funny without getting in trouble for it, where he could, in fact, win a five dollar prize just for telling jokes.

Gleason worked carnivals and water shows, tried prize fighting, pool hustling and exhibition diving among other things, before he began playing gangsters and sailors in Warner Bros movies at the age of 25. The man who would one day be known the world over as 'The Great One' began his career with bit parts in forgettable movies. He had lines such as, 'It's time to get back to the ship.' He once said of his early movie days, 'They paid me 250 a week, but I had to provide my own ammunition.'

From there he made his way to Broadway. It was during the run of **Along Fifth Avenue** in 1949 when Gleason, like so many other future stars, made his television debut on Ed Sullivan's **Toast of the Town**. Contrary to popular opinion, Elvis Presley did *not* debut on Ed Sullivan,

**Opposite page: With a suit as loud as his mouth, Jackie Gleason began each weekly installment of his variety program, The Jackie Gleason Show, with his signature rallying cry, 'And away we go!'**

**Opposite left:** Young stand-up comic and bit player Jackie Gleason holds the phone in this early publicity still.

**At right:** One of Gleason's favorite characters on *Cavalcade of Stars* was Joe the Bartender. The skits were performed as monologues, with Joe greeting and trading barbs with unseen customers, most of them named for his old friends from Bushwick.

but instead on Gleason's **Stage Show**, where he was shown from head to toe. Gleason's cameramen didn't censor the King's swivel.

That same year, after his appearance on **Toast of the Town**, Jackie began appearing on television as the first Chester A Riley in NBC's **Life of Riley**. William Bendix created the character on the radio and brought it to television, but was unavailable that year due to previous commitments. Legend has it that Bendix was fired because an appliance manufacturer was not willing to sponsor a show whose star had the name of a rival washing machine, but the sponsor was actually Pabst Brewing.

In any event, Jackie seemed uncomfortable in the prefabricated role. Also, the blue collar comedy and was not filmed before an audience and had no laugh track, which gave the show a somber mood. After the first season, the show won an Emmy, but after 26 episodes, Pabst Brewing dropped the show and began sponsoring prize fights instead. Gleason went back to performing stand-up in nightclubs and other live venues.

Gleason's gigs ranged in pay anywhere from $150 for a radio program to $3000 for a week at the Roxie in New York City. He was working at Los Angeles' most famous night club, Slapsie Maxie's, when an offer came in to return to television, on a show called **Cavalcade of Stars**. The producer wanted someone to tie the show together, someone who could emcee **and** perform in sketches.

*Above:* Gleason 'discovered' Art Carney, a tap dancer and impressionist, when he was playing a waiter on another show, Morey Amsterdam's *The Silver Swan Café.* They formed what was to be a lifelong personal and professional alliance.

With their scripts on the counter, they rehearse for a 'Loudmouth Charlie' Bratton sketch in which Loudmouth Charlie will once again ruin Art Carney's lunch.

*Opposite page:* Joe the Bartender was based on Mr Dennehy, the owner of Proce's Bar in Gleason's old neighborhood of Bushwick, New York. Joe always said hello to 'Mr Dennehy' as well as other real-life friends of Gleason's — Jackie's way of letting his old pals know he was still thinking of them.

Gleason didn't see any reason why he should leave his job on the West Coast to go do television for two weeks, especially when his previous television experience had not been very good. The DuMont network offered Jackie four weeks instead, and he agreed, saying that he was doing it for the money. He left California fully expecting to be back within the month.

Gleason became the guest emcee on DuMont's *Cavalcade of Stars*. The show was a one-hour weekly variety show, run on a shoe-string, used by various comedians to tighten up their acts and gain some exposure. Jack Carter, Larry Storch and Jerry Lester had all emceed the show and moved on.

Television at this time was similar to movies in the 1930s, with a profusion of show girls, comedians and production extravaganzas. When sound revolutionized the movies, film makers reveled in the expanded possibility of and dancing *and* singing. Later, the addition of image on the home screen had much the same effect: lots of singing and dancing. It was just the sort of entertainment that needed Jackie's kind of showmanship.

In those early days of the new medium, few headlining celebrities would perform on television. For one thing, they risked nation-wide failure if the appearance was a bust. Television shows didn't pay well enough to justify that kind of risk. And material that would last a

The character of the Poor Soul *(at left)*, which Gleason performed entirely in mime, was certainly an oddity amongst Gleason's other less timorous creations such as Reginald Van Gleason III *(at right)*.

performer for years on the live performance circuit was usually burned up in fifteen minutes on the gamma ray circuit. But Gleason was ready to put his talent to the test.

When Gleason first arrived, the producer and director took him around the set to show him how things would be done. Gleason instead told *them* how *he* would be doing things. Ever since he had started in show business, he had carefully observed every detail that went into production, and he was ready and determined to command his own show. He wanted to fail or succeed according to his own merits.

Jackie wanted elegance and beautiful women (he hand-picked the June Taylor Dancers), and both comic and serious sketches.
Jackie decided that the tiny budget of **Cavalcade** would no longer be spent on 'name' guest stars, but that instead he would develop his own cast of characters: Joe the Bartender, Reginald Van Gleason III, Stanley R Sogg, the Poor Soul, loudmouthed Charlie Bratton (inspired by Gleason's own 'Uncle Fat'), Rudy the Repairman, and eventually, Ralph Kramden. These characters all resurfaced later on **The Jackie Gleason Show**.

*These pages:* **After he found fame as Subterranean Sanitation Engineer Ed Norton, Art Carney didn't need his friends to pull any strings for him to obtain future acting jobs. Here, Carney is shown with the puppets from the children's classic, *Peter and the Wolf.***

The show was hilarious. Jim Bishop wrote in his biography of Gleason, **The Golden Ham**,

On the opening night of **Cavalcade of Stars**, Jackie…was so funny that even the writers laughed. In one sketch, there was a Dutch half-closed door that Gleason was supposed to exit through. The door got stuck. Gleason climbed over it. The audience giggled. When he had to make another entrance, Jackie climbed over it as though that were the way a Dutch door was intended to be used. The audience roared. He went in and out and over that door so many times that people were weak from laughter. Even the camera crews roared. The network wondered if Gleason could be that funny twice in a row.

For the second show, Gleason hired an actor, tap dancer and impressionist named Art Carney to appear in sketches and act as announcer. He had noticed Carney on Morey Amsterdam's **The Silver Swan Café**, playing a waiter. Recognized as an 'actor's actor' by talented performers such as Katharine Hepburn and Alfred Lunt, Art Carney, in his first appearance on **Cavalcade of Stars**, was a fussy, persnickety photographer—not unlike Felix Unger, the character he later created on Broadway in Neil Simon's **The Odd Couple**.

In the sketch, a photographer is assigned to photograph Reggie Van Gleason III for a 'Distinguished Profile' liquor ad. Van Gleason sports top hat and opera cape, a cane, a moustache and the exaggerated gestures of a spoiled swell. Reggie takes swigs from the sponsor's bottle and starts to misbehave. The photographer, in exasperation, takes a drink and tries to get on with the shooting. Soon, both of them are reeling, the photo shoot and the feud forgotten.

# THE HONEYMOON BEGINS

**W**hile working with writers on the third show, Jackie suggested that they do a sketch based less on caricature, and more on real characters, set in a familiar domestic situation. Jackie laid out the bare bones: a married couple, without much money. The husband is loud and blustery, the wife is quiet, but not unarmed. Jackie went on to say that they fight all the time, but 'they always end in a clinch.' He described the wife as 'very wise and very tired.'

When he first suggested the name 'The Honeymooners,' the writers, Joe Bigelow and Harry Crane, protested that it sounded too lovey-dovey. But that was just the kind of left-handed humor that Gleason was looking for: it conveyed sarcastically that they're *not* always lovey-dovey, and that their relationship really hasn't changed since they were first married. They still have, and probably always will have, the same quarrels and problems. And yet the truth is that the couple really does love one another.

Gleason had already been formulating **The Honeymooners** in his mind for years. Growing up, he had heard this kind of fighting through the walls of the Brooklyn apartments where he and his mother lived. He was full of ideas. That same writing session, Gleason began to describe a third or fourth floor cold-water flat, on Flatbush Avenue in Brooklyn. He described where the icebox would go, and the inevitable drip pan beneath it. The sideboard, the gas range and the round table—Gleason said, 'Hell, I lived in these joints.'

Ralph and Alice first appeared on 22 July 1950, Jackie's third week of hosting **Cavalcade of Stars**. The sketch was only a few minutes long. Trixie and Ed were not yet invented, and Pert Kelton played Alice. It had been proposed that Ralph be a policeman, but the idea was rejected because a policeman has some degree of authority over the outside world. Ralph Kramden is a man whose only 'castle' is his home, if that.

In this first episode, Ralph came home from driving the bus and Alice asked him to go downstairs for a loaf of bread. Ralph went into a rage about how he'd been at work all day, and then he was expected to run to the store. Alice responded that she'd been busy, too, and showed him

**Opposite page: A cornerstone of *The Honeymooners* was the contentious yet compatible friendship between Ralph Kramden and his neighbor Norton. Their big dreams and schemes usually brought them nothing but trouble.**

the pie that she made. The argument escalated, and Ralph threw the pie at Alice. Alice ducked, and the pie flew out the window. Ralph and Alice continued to argue, until a knock came at the door. It was Art Carney as a neighborhood cop, covered in pie. With one leg slung over the sill, Alice threatened to jump out the window, and Ralph said, 'Go ahead and jump.' Alice replied, 'I wouldn't give you the satisfaction.'

**The Honeymooners** sketches continued to be rotated into the **Cavalcade** lineup, along with Jackie's other regular skits. Whenever they did a **Honeymooners** skit, the ratings went up. The character of Norton, Ralph's sidekick, was created for Art Carney. Then Gleason decided that Norton needed a wife.

In the 1950s, Joyce Randolph was working with some of the most famous names in television, such as Fred Allen, Jerry Lewis and Dean Martin. She had first appeared on **Cavalcade of Stars** in a serious role. She played opposite Jackie in a poignant story of two lovers reunited in a backstage dressing room after many years' separation. When Gleason needed to find Ed Norton a wife, he said, 'Get me that serious

*These pages: A common set-up was Gleason as the cigar-chomping garrulous buffoon and Carney as the fastidious, bespectacled victim, somewhat like the character of Felix Unger whom he later developed on Broadway.*

*The warmth and chemistry between the two actors was apparent in their scenes together. Below, Gleason attempts to keep a straight face as Carney lets his face go rubbery.*

actress.' Trixie, the former burlesque queen, was born, and Joyce Randolph joined the cast of **The Honeymooners**.

## Success

Ratings on **Cavalcade** went from a nine to a 25 percent average share of the audience. Another network, hoping to cut into Jackie's lion share, scheduled **Cavalcade of Sports** (the fights) in their Friday night 10:00-11:00 slot. Proce's, the neighborhood bar which was the source of much of the material in Gleason's Joe the Bartender skits, had to install another television set to avoid their *own* fights over program selection.

The phenomenal popularity of a television show has something to do with the time in history in which it is aired. Just about everyone watching television in the 1950s could remember being poor, or at least tight. They could sympathize with Ralph's dream of winning money on a game show, or Alice's desire to have a telephone, as attested to by the hundreds of curtains and other niceties sent to Alice in the mail. The continuing success of **The Honeymooners** today, despite the fact that only 39 episodes remain, is what truly marks it as a classic.

*Right:* Carney continued to act on other shows whenever his *Honeymooners* schedule would allow it. Here he appears on *The General Electric Theatre* in a teleplay entitled, 'Hooray for Love.'

*Opposite page:* Gleason sailed into his first television program, *Cavalcade of Stars*, taking on the responsibilities of emceeing, producing, writing and starring on the hour-long show, as well as keeping an eye on lighting, wardrobe and other facets of this hit show.

Jackie Gleason was in charge of producing an hour of stellar entertainment every week, and he demanded perfection from everyone on the staff. He went through more writers more quickly than probably anyone else in the history of show business. He began on **Cavalcade** with Arne Rosen and Coleman Jacoby. Harry Crane and Joe Bigelow soon joined the team. Harry became head writer and the others moved on. Marvin Marx was hired, and he in turn persuaded Walter Stone to sign on. Stone was reluctant because he had heard of Jackie's hire-and-fire reputation, but then decided to give it a try. By the time Stone got there, Marx had been fired. Later, Stone brought Marx back to write with him.

In 1951, Jackie checked himself into a hospital for a monitored weight-loss diet. The writers, seeing their advantage in Jackie's captivity, sat and wrote two shows with him in one week. Jackie was duly impressed. He kept that team with him for the duration of the Dumont contact and took them with him when he moved to CBS to do **The Jackie Gleason Show** in 1952. Walter Stone and Marvin Marx (until his death in the mid-seventies) were still writing **The Honeymooners** specials 30

*Opposite page:* **Trixie Norton (Joyce Randolph), former burlesque queen and lifelong blonde, waits for husband Ed (Art Carney) to dole out some grocery money. The rest of the Nortons' purchases were made on time.**

*Above:* **Norton has been fishing around the Kramdens' icebox while Ralph holds his fishing pole.**

years after the Kramdens were created. The quality of the scripts was largely attributed to this pair, because, according to executive producer Jack Philbin, Marx thought like Ralph, Stone thought like Norton.

Gleason threw out even very funny scripts if he thought that they weren't true to the characters. And he would know. Real names and addresses from Jackie's youth in Bushwick are sprinkled liberally throughout **The Honeymooners**, though transplanted to Bensonhurst because that neighborhood has a more recognizable name. Gleason lived on Chauncey Street. The Kramdens' cat-owning neighbor was based on Jackie's real-life neighbor; Mr Dennehy of the 'Joe the Bartender' skits was Jackie's neighbor and friend down at Proce's Bar (another example of art imitating life). Ralph's boss down at the Gotham Bus Company, JJ Marshall, is named for Gleason's first girlfriend, Julie Dennehy, and her husband, J Marshall.

Jackie was a perfectionist, and he exercised his right to veto scripts. Once he turned down all ten scripts that the writers had prepared over the summer. One week, no script turned up at all. Jackie didn't worry, though. That afternoon, with only four-and-a-half hours until air time, he brought Pert and Art back to his hotel room to bang out a script. They decided to have cocktails before they started. They never started. They continued to have cocktails until twenty minutes before the curtain

*Left:* **Jackie Gleason welcomes the audience to *The Jackie Gleason Show* in the costume of his most famous character, Ralph Kramden. Ralph almost always appeared in one of his two uniforms: a bus-driver's or a Raccoon's.**

*Above:* **Gleason is the man credited with selling most Americans their first television. This forward-thinking couple even has a remote control.**

went up. On the way to the studio, they agreed upon this bare premise: Alice and Ralph would bicker. Norton would come in, and make it all worse. The sponsor was in a state of shock. Before millions of people on live television, Jackie, Pert and Art winged it.

After the show, the three went back to a dressing room and waited to get fired. Instead, the sponsor congratulated them on their funniest show yet.

In July of 1952, with their DuMont contract running out, the Honeymooners went on a four-show-a-day tour of major cities. They broke records everywhere they went. Pert seemed to be dragging somewhat, unable to keep up with the enthusiastic drinking that went on all night after performing all day.

One day she went on as Alice, and left the stage mid-argument to get sick. Then Pert came right back out and picked up the fight with Ralph. The audience went wild, not knowing that Pert wasn't faking it. Even the cast and crew thought she was simply feeling the aftermath of a night of drinking. By the end of the day, however, she had collapsed. Diagnosed with coronary thrombosis, Pert finished the tour, but could not possibly continue to appear on the show. Once back in New York, Gleason had to find a new Alice.

# CHANGING CHANNELS

**J**ackie Gleason had long since outgrown the DuMont network. He was now a big star, 'The Great One', and DuMont was not a big network. Guest appearances on other networks were bringing him $12,500 *per appearance*, while DuMont was hardly sharing the wealth that Jackie generated for them. He had begun on **Cavalcade of Stars** with a $5000 *loan* from the network. His salary had finally risen to $1,500 a week. After the managers, agents and staff had dipped in, however, with $450 taken out against the loan, as little as $90 was left over for Jackie. One week, when Jackie couldn't perform because he was sick with a toothache and could barely speak, the network refused to pay him at all.

After two years on DuMont, Jackie took Art Carney, Joyce Randolph and the June Taylor Dancers and defected to CBS. There, he took even greater control of the show, which would this time bear his name, **The Jackie Gleason Show**. Jackie owned, produced, and was solely responsible for the one hour variety show. He hired the orchestra, the writers, the dancers and the cast. In addition to producing, directing and starring, Jackie performed thousands of uncredited chores: he worked with the lighting and the editing, and selected some of the most beautiful dancers. He even helped choose their costumes. He also wrote the theme song, and other musical compositions for the show.

When Jackie took charge, Joyce Randolph was given a raise, and a steady income whether she appeared on the show or not. When Art Carney's agent demanded $750 a week, Gleason suggested $1,000. Art accepted. Now all Jackie had to do was find a new Alice.

A rising young actress, Audrey Meadows was considered one of the most beautiful and glamorous women in New York, so when Jackie Gleason heard that she was interested in the role of Alice, he didn't even consider her. She knew she could play the part, so she tried to look frumpy, but she couldn't quite pull it off. Finally, she hired a photographer to wake her up at 5:30 in the morning and take her picture first thing. When Gleason saw those photographs, he exclaimed, 'Jeez, you really are a dowdy broad!' She got the part.

*Opposite page:* **Many fans regretted that when Gleason changed the format of his one-hour *Jackie Gleason Show* to a half-hour of *The Honeymooners*, he would no longer give a weekly welcome to the audience with one of his wonderful monologues. Occasionally, the cast of *The Honeymooners* would step out of character to greet the audience or to wish them a Merry Christmas.**

*Left:* **The picture of marital bliss, Jackie Gleason (Ralph) and Audrey Meadows (Alice) act like honeymooners.**

*Below, right:* **By the glint in his eye, one can tell that this Subterranean Sanitation Engineer really loves his job.**

## *Chauncey Street History*

With all of the players in place, the Kramdens and the Nortons revealed more of their own personal histories with each episode. Ralph Kramden, born in Brooklyn, had gotten his start delivering groceries for the Atlantic & Pacific Tea Company, then began shoveling snow for the WPA. His Uncle Leo wanted him to study architecture, but Ralph gave it up to learn the Charleston instead. He met Alice Gibson while working at the WPA, and eventually married her and began driving a bus on the Madison Avenue route of the Gotham Bus Company. His Social Security number is 105-36-22 (possibly the only seven-digit Social Security number in the country). He and his best friend, Edward L Norton, are both Raccoons and both bowl on lane number three.

Norton grew up in Oyster Bay, attended PS 31, majored in arithmetic in vocational school, and worked as a caddy during the Depression. When he followed a golf ball down a sewer, he got the job that eventually led to his position as an Engineer in Subterranean Sanitation. The sergeant-at-arms for the Raccoon Lodge, he has held the honor of Raccoon of the Year, and serves as a ranger third class in the Captain Video Space Academy.

Not much is known about Ed's wife, Trixie Norton. A former burlesque queen, she has always been blonde. She can't cook, and Ed says

*These pages:* **Fare is fare, and even wives and friends must pay when the driver is honest Ralph Kramden.**

*These pages:* **During their infrequent rehearsals, Audrey Meadows always wore her costume, in an attempt to prevent on-air mistakes such as props missing from apron pockets.**

that's why he no longer looks like Clark Gable. She and Ed buy things on time.

Alice's past also remains somewhat obscure, though more is known about her family than the other characters'. Her maiden name is Gibson. Her sister, Agnes, is married to Ralph's lodge brother, Stanley Saxon. Her mother, Ralph's mother-in-law, mean Mrs Gibson, lives alternately in Astoria in Queens and at 33 Kosciusko Street in Brooklyn. Mrs Gibson maintains that Alice should have married her old suitor who is still thin and handsome. She regrets that Alice gave up a good job in a laundry to marry Ralph.

The neighbors at 328 Chauncey Street are a continual source of annoyance for the Kramdens, and vice versa. Mrs Manicotti, her husband and her son Tommy live upstairs, as do crotchety Mr Garrity and, of course, the Nortons. Mrs Schwartz is the building gossip. Mr Murphy lives alone. He had to drink warm beer for months after Mrs Murphy ran off with the iceman.

## Civil War Style

There were times when Audrey Meadows wished she had never heard of Jackie Gleason. She suffered terribly under the stresses of his anarchic production style. The show was live, and Jackie didn't believe

in what he called 'over-rehearsing.' His photographic memory allowed him to read over a 60-page script on Saturday morning and know it for that night's performance. Adamantly refusing cue cards, he once recorded 20 commercials in a row in under 15 minutes without a mistake. He'd go through the motions of a dress rehearsal for the sake of the others, sometimes merely reading through the lines with the other cast members in his penthouse at the Park Central Hotel. He liked the spontaneity and freshness generated by the actors' lack of exposure to the material. He always said that the first time a line is said is the funniest.

Freshness and spontaneity could translate into panic and chaos, but the audience never seemed to notice. The associate director of the show, Kenneth Whelan, claimed that the guy who delivered the coffee knew as much as he did about what was going on, and that the stage hands were the best informed people around. They, at least, knew what the new sets looked like each week.

During Audrey Meadows' first week on the show, she kept asking when they were going to rehearse. By show time, she was 'psychopathic with fright.' 'I felt totally unprepared and desperate. Standing in the wings, ready to go on, I'd tell him, "You are a simply dreadful man!"' She pulled it off on pure adrenaline.

**Above: Ralph warns Alice for the umpteenth time that, one of these days, he is going to send her 'to the Moon!'**

**Opposite page: Art Carney, Jackie Gleason and Audrey Meadows became close friends despite working under the stressful conditions engendered by Jackie's 'Civil War style' of shooting the show.**

Audrey learned that if her cue never came, she should walk in anyway. Jackie called the productions 'Civil War style.' Among the soldiers, there was some in-fighting. Whenever The Great One forgot a line, he had a signal: he'd pat his stomach and let one of the others think of something. Usually, Audrey Meadows would say what was on her mind. Some of Alice's biggest insults were created that way. One night she snapped, 'If you get any bigger, gasbag, you'll just float away.'

In an early ***Honeymooners*** episode, Alice was supposed to serve Ralph a frozen steak, which he would then whack angrily and knock to the floor. There was no rehearsal, and no one told Jackie or Audrey that the 'steak' was made out of wood. When Jackie hit the prop, the steak cracked in half, with one piece flying off the set. With twenty million people watching the live broadcast, Gleason glared at her, waiting for her to save the scene. Audrey simply said, 'There you are, Ralph. Tonight I'm serving you *half* of a steak!'

Another time, Jackie was supposed to throw a pie at Audrey. They hadn't rehearsed, and Audrey knew he'd miss by two feet. At the critical moment when Jackie wound up to throw, she pretended to stumble and threw herself in the path of the flying pie, saving yet another scene. She earned the title of 'the Rock' because of her seeming calm in such situations.

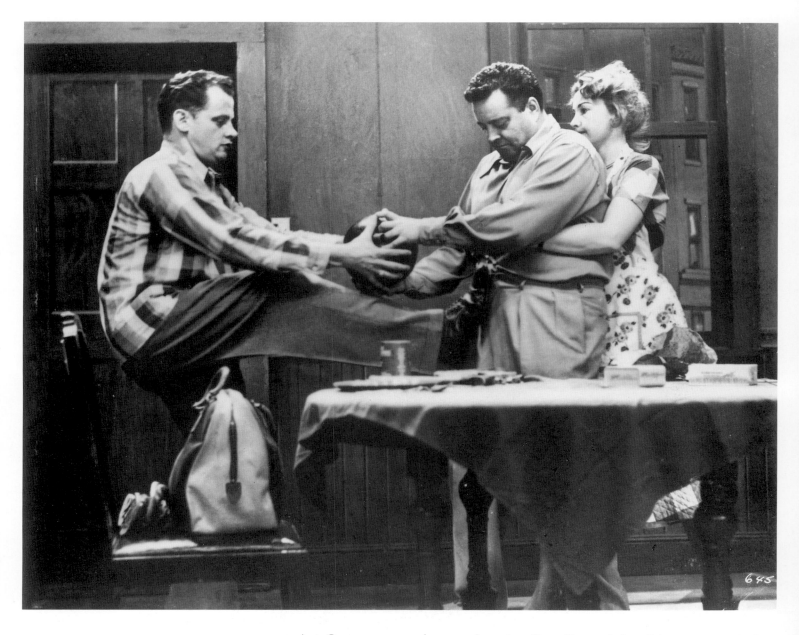

Art Carney was also cool under fire. One night, Gleason made his exit through the bedroom door and made one of his rare mistakes. He forgot that he had to come back on stage. According to the script, Alice was supposed to get him and bring him right back on stage. She exited through the bedroom door, leaving Art Carney alone on stage. But backstage, Audrey couldn't find Jackie. He had wandered off, thinking he had more time than he did.

Art Carney was left alone on stage, with a live telecast going out to millions of people. He had no idea why the others had abandoned him like this. He didn't falter for a second. He made his way to the icebox, found an orange, and for the next two minutes he sat at the kitchen table and peeled it. He didn't say a word. Kenneth Whelan called it 'the funniest two minutes I'd ever seen.'

Audrey finally found Jackie and returned to the stage, but Whelan was convinced that Art could have gone on improvising for hours, alone on an almost empty stage, and kept the audience laughing.

Even when the show was being taped for broadcast later, if the set wall came down on **The Jackie Gleason Show**, the cameras rolled. Doors would stick, and Art Carney would simply come in the window. Occasionally, the cameras had to stop and do another take, when a cast member accidentally slipped out a word not suitable for younger viewers.

*Left:* **Art Carney, Jackie Gleason and Audrey Meadows rehearse a slapstick routine in which Ralph's fingers become stuck in his bowling ball, and Norton and Alice must pull him loose.**

*Below, right:* **Jackie as Ralph Kramden in front of the CBS cameras for *The Jackie Gleason Show*.**

On 30 January 1954, Gleason slipped and fell on stage, dislocating his foot, tearing ligaments and fracturing his leg. Gleason casually got himself out of the scene and off the stage and down to the hospital. The audience, howling with laughter, thought Jackie had just taken a pratfall, but it was close to two months before his return.

Until Jackie's recovery, guest hosts such as Ed Sullivan, Red Skelton and Eddie Fisher took the helm. Two weeks after the accident, the audience was begging for more **Honeymooners**, so Art Carney took the world into Norton's apartment for the first time, for a satire of Edward R Murrow's **Person to Person**.

For Jackie's much anticipated return on 23 March, Jackie backed a **Honeymooners** sketch with his own arrangements of 'romantic jazz,' and even conducted the 40-piece Ray Bloch orchestra himself.

For all his procrastination and nonchalance, Gleason was undeniably a genius, and he, Art and Audrey were devoted to each other. Art Carney said that because of his faith in Gleason, 'We've never had a fight, never as much as a cross word.' And Audrey, who once gave Gleason 'The World's Largest Martini Shaker,' said, 'You can't look bad when you're in a scene with Gleason. He's that good.'

# IN REAL LIFE

**H**erbert John 'Jackie' Gleason's father had disappeared when he was nine. His mother, Mae, left to support herself and her son, died nine years later. *The Honeymooners* set would be based on the half dozen homes that Jackie and Mae lived in before settling on Chauncey Street. Known for his fast ad-libs and brash humor, Jackie won his first amateur contest at the age of fifteen at the Halsey Theatre. Jack Warner discovered Gleason for the movies at Club 18 in New York. He made five films in Hollywood, then returned to New York to work on Broadway. He made his television debut on Ed Sullivan's *Toast of the Town*, then appeared in many television plays, including 'The Laugh Maker' on *Studio One* with Art Carney. He also composed music, including *Tawny*, a tone poem/ballet.

Gleason starred in the movies *Gigot* and *The Hustler*, receiving an Academy Award nomination for his role as Minnesota Fats in the latter. The following year, 1962, he starred in the movie, *Requiem for a Heavyweight*. He then returned to television to do *The Jackie Gleason Show: The American Scene Magazine*, a comedy/satire variety show. He starred in the movies, *Papa's Delicate Condition* (1963), *How to Commit Marriage* (1969) and *Don't Drink the Water* (1969). In the early 1980s, Gleason appeared in a television movie with Sir Lawrence Olivier called *Mr Halpern and Mr Johnson*. Gleason and Carney reunited on television for *Izzy and Moe*, the true story of two Prohibition-era cops.

Jackie Gleason's homes were always monuments to the good life. An architect designed a unique $800,000 (in 1976 dollars) abode in Peekskill, New York, for the Great One. Round like Gleason himself, his house looked like a giant spaceship. Inside were a dozen bars, pool tables and round-the-clock crap games. His home in Florida had a wing on the house named 'Gleason's Pool Hall' — a 40' x 60' air conditioned room filled with pool tables.

Before she won her role as Alice Kramden, **Audrey Meadows** appeared in *Bob and Ray* and *Alfred Hitchcock Presents*. She worked with Phil Silvers in *Top Banana*, and appeared in Broadway theatre. She appeared in motion pictures with James Stewart and Cary Grant. After *The Honeymooners*, she appeared with Red Skelton, Jack Benny, George Gobel, Carol Burnett and Sid Caesar, as well as straight

*Opposite page: Jackie got an opportunity to shoot some stick when he portrayed real-life pool great Minnesota Fats in the 1961 movie, The Hustler, starring Paul Newman. Gleason received an Academy Award nomination for Best Supporting Actor.*

**Left:** Audrey Meadows had her hands full working for Continental Airlines and running a bank in Denver when she rejoined the gang on two *Honeymooners* specials in the late 1970s.

**Right:** Art Carney went on to win an Academy Award for his first starring movie role in *Harry and Tonto* (1975).

dramatic performances on almost every major television playhouse production.

She later married Robert Six, board chairman of Continental Air Services, and more or less retired from show business. She did return for **The Honeymooners**' 25th Anniversary show in 1976, as well as the two specials in 1977 and 1978. When she left Hollywood behind, she became the first woman director of the First National Bank of Denver. She also served as honorary vice president of sales for Continental Airlines.

Born in Mt Vernon, New York, **Art Carney** was an impressionist and tap dancer who made his debut at an Elks Club in the 1930s. In the 40s, he became active in radio, on daytime serials, mysteries, spot recordings and children's shows. On a serious political program called **Report to the Nation**, he did the voices of prominent figures of the day such as Roosevelt and Churchill. He worked with Morey Amsterdam on a radio program that began appearing on television. Thus, Carney began working on television. He appeared in television specials such as **Suspense**, **Harvey**, **Burlesque**, **Kraft Theatre**, **Climax**, **Charlie's Aunt**, **Playhouse 90** and **Studio One**. Without a single acting lesson, he won an Oscar for his first starring movie role, playing Harry in the 1975 film, **Harry and Tonto**. His other film appearances include **A Guide for the Married Man**, **WW and the Dixie Dance Kings**, and **The Late Show**.

# HAR-DEE HAR-HAR-HAR

**M**eanwhile, the well-ensconced competition on the other networks were losing ground against *The Jackie Gleason Show*. Jimmy Durante's *All-Star Revue* featured a no-holds-barred barrage one week, to try to defend their claim on the Saturday night 10 o'clock slot. Despite the Schnozz's team of ringers—including Groucho Marx, Milton Berle, Ethel Barrymore and Martha Raye—Jackie won the ratings war.

In July 1954, *The Jackie Gleason Show* came in third in the American Research Bureau's ratings of weekly programs at a 41.4. *I Love Lucy* was first, on CBS, with 56.8, and *Dragnet* came in with 41.9. Six months later, Jackie *et al* had edged out the competition with a 53.4 percent of homes reached. Eleven hundred people each week camped out starting early Saturday in order to be members of the audience for the broadcast performance. Hundreds of aprons and curtains came in the mail each week from people who wanted Alice's existence to be less drab. She even received potholders from a bank who promised that if she banked with them, Ralph would never have to know. The show was a phenomenon. Then it was contract renewal time.

## The Big Buick Contract

Jackie's contract for the 1955-1956 season was the biggest ever negotiated for a performer in the history of show business. Buick dropped 'Mr Television,' Milton Berle, in favor of Gleason, 'Mr Saturday Night' as their new representative. Milton Berle learned of his dismissal when he read a trade paper on the way to rehearsals of his program.

The show was restructered, along with the contract. Ralph, Alice, Trixie and Ed would receive their own half hour, and Gleason's production company, jackie gleason enterprises, inc (always with lower case) would fill the second half hour. Under the new negotiations, Jackie would make as much for the half hour of *The Honeymooners* as he had previously for the entire hour of *The Jackie Gleason Show*, in addition to making money for filling the other time slot.

**Opposite page: In a typical scene from the Kramden household, Ralph is glib, Norton is shocked and Alice stands firm.**

*Above:* **Ralph and Alice have their differences, but their arguments usually end with Ralph taking Alice in his arms and telling her, 'Baby, you're the greatest.'**

*Opposite page:* **Ralph's bowling was a common source of friction between him and Alice, who complained of having to stay home without even a television to watch while Ralph and Norton went bowling on lane number three and to meetings at the Raccoon Lodge. 'I want to look at Liberace,' she complained.**

Buick paid Jackie $65,000 for each of the next season's 39 episodes. The show went to film at this time, giving Gleason a product which he could sell after the original airing. In fact, this contract helped begin the trend toward filming television series. Jackie made a deal for reruns in the summer of 1956, and received an additional $32,500 for each of the thirteen reruns. For the second year of his contract, Jackie was to receive $70,000 per episode, as well as $35,000 per rerun. Out of these enormous sums of money, Jackie had to pay all production costs, including the salaries of his friends and co-stars, Art Carney and Audrey Meadows.

The contract also stipulated that Gleason would continue to receive a salary from CBS after his Buick contract expired, so long as he promised not to make any deals with other networks.

Jackie and *The Honeymooners* were now in the spotlight, making them the target of critics and fans alike, who were now more critical. A number of articles queried whether anyone could possibly be worth that much money, and whether or not the show was losing its charm now that it was filmed. Since he had usurped the king of television comedy, Milton Berle, the network used Jackie and his publicity as their greatest weapon, positioning the show against their toughest competition: Perry Como on ABC and Jimmy Durante on NBC.

He and Berle had never really been friends, a situation exacerbated by professional competition. Milton Berle had a habit of grabbing people by the arm in a friendly manner, then edging them out of the spotlight. One night when Jackie and 'Uncle Miltie' were to perform together, Berle tried this trick and recoiled in pain. Too late he saw the row of pins bristling out of Jackie's sleeve. Another night when Gleason was performing with Phil Silvers, Berle began to heckle them from ringside. Gleason pinned Berle to the floor while a friend poured water on Berle's head.

The rest of the cast profited as well from the new deal. Art Carney was earning $3500 a week, Audrey Meadows $2000, and Joyce Randolph, who appeared in approximately three-quarters of the filmed episodes, $500.

The entire team realized, however, that they now had to be $11 million worth of funny.

Gleason used to say that an entertainer should work hard enough during his performance that the average person in the audience would say, 'You couldn't give me a million dollars to do that.' Their stage show at the Paramount Theatre in 1954 was another example of Jackie's capacity for hard work. The entire **Honeymooners** cast continued to do their regular weekly broadcasts of **The Jackie Gleason Show** in addi-

*These pages:* **Perhaps the most famous photograph of the cast of** *The Honeymooners* **features Ralph taking Alice, Ed and Trixie for a ride on the Gotham Bus Company line.**

tion to doing live shows every day. When someone asked Audrey Meadows if they could get her anything, she replied, 'Yes, a cake with a file in it.'

## The Classic ElectroniCam 39

During the September 1955-September 1956 season, 39 shows were performed before an audience and recorded simultaneously with the magic of the 'ElectroniCam,' a technology developed by DuMont Laboratories to capitalize on syndication possibilities while preserving the look of a live telecast. Two cameras were mounted side-by-side on a base, sharing the same lens. One camera was a television camera which provided the quality of the image, and the other provided the director, the editor, choreographer, lighting, makeup and wardrobe experts with a duplicate image to watch during filming. Previously only the cameraman had been able to see what the finished product would look like.

The entire show took less than forty minutes to film, including one break in the middle to change film magazines. The producers thereby saved huge amounts of money compared to the conventional filming method, which usually required three to four days to shoot one show. Gleason knew that audiences at home often felt 'tricked' by filmed broadcasts, so on **The Honeymooners**, every effort was made to pre-

*These pages: Jackie Gleason, Art Carney and Audrey Meadows in a holiday episode of The Honeymooners.*

serve the spontaneity of a live broadcast. Nothing was reshot, and the orchestra played along, even though the music was later dubbed in. The audience's response was never augmented by canned laughter.

The first ElectroniCam episode, which aired 1 October 1955, is now regarded as a classic. Alice decides that she wants a television. She is tired of looking at the icebox, the stove, the sink and four walls while Ralph and Norton go out bowling, playing pool or to the Raccoon Lodge. She wants to look at Liberace. The conclusion of the story is that Alice and Ralph both realize they were better off without a television.

The production costs of that first show were $75,000, twice the cost of either **I Love Lucy** or **Alfred Hitchcock Presents**. Despite the increase in budget, the new technology and the fact that these programs would be preserved forever, rehearsal time was still kept at the minimum. Cast, crew and writers turned out episodes at the rate of two a week.

Many factors were responsible for the show's enormous popularity. Just to name two: Jackie Gleason's instincts for keeping the show true to character, and his protectiveness toward the script quality of the shows. For example, 'The Bensonhurst Bunny Club' was a 1960s episode in which Ralph devises a get-rich-quick scheme: he and Norton will raise rabbits for fur coats and sell them as minks. The script was done, and even all the words and music for an hour-long musical had been completed by Lyn Duddy and Jerry Bresler. But Jackie thought about Norton and Ralph skinning little bunnies and decided to kill the show.

# RALPH AND FRIENDS

The character of Ralph Kramden is somehow lovable despite himself. Ralph is elements of all the Gleason characters rolled into one: Charlie Bratton's loud mouth, the Poor Soul's dejection, even the pretension—when Ralph is feeling insecure—of Reginald Van Gleason III. Ralph is almost always seen in uniform, either that of a Raccoon or bus driver. He is not a man who looks good in uniform. He is a loudmouth combination of stock phrases such as 'Har-har-har-dee-har-har,' 'One of these days, right on the kisser,' 'Baby, you're the greatest,' and the famous 'To the moon, Alice, to the moon.'

But the audience loves him, as do his wife and best friend. Those two relationships form the crux of the show, and are the most important elements in Ralph's life. No matter how much he and Alice argue, or how much Norton gets on his nerves, by the end of the show Alice is 'the greatest' and Norton is, well, Norton.

Norton, of course, is almost always seen in his white t-shirt, vest and battered felt hat—a hat that Art Carney bought when he was in high school in Yonkers, New York.

Norton's abilities are revealed as they are needed by Ralph. When Ralph's category on **The $99,000 Question** is popular music, Norton offers to help Ralph. Ralph discovers, after 14 years of friendship, that Norton can read music and play piano well. When Ralph may have to fight a bully, Norton reveals his previously undisclosed boxing skills to spar with Ralph. The phrase 'second banana' was created for Carney by the CBS executives.

Norton has had some successes in his life away from Ralph. At the lodge, he is sergeant-at-arms and Raccoon of the Year. He is a Video Ranger, third class, in the Captain Video Space Academy. In the episode entitled 'The Safety Award', Ed is recognized for his poem to promote sewer safety:

'When the tides of life turn against you
And the current upsets your boat
Don't waste those tears on what might have been;
Just lay on your back and float.'

**Opposite page: Ralph Kramden believes that a man's home is his castle and his bus is his trusty steed.**

The friendship between Ralph and Norton is one of the cornerstones of the show. Norton and Ralph are like Laurel and Hardy—who inci-

*Left:* **Ed Norton (Art Carney) looks down the stairwell from the floor above the Kramdens at 328 Chauncey Street.**

*Below, right:* **Like millions of fans, these women have put Art Carney up on a pedestal.**

dentally were among their most devoted fans — the gullible, skinny one and the blustery, self-important fat blowhard. They get into the same sort of scrapes as Laurel and Hardy: financial schemes, botched deceptions, fights with bullies, and petty disputes. Norton and Ralph even dress up in Laurel and Hardy costumes for a bus company party.

Norton gets his jibes in at Ralph, especially in terms of fat jokes. 'Below the belt' is no small target on Ralph. When Ralph and Norton have an argument in 'The Man From Space', Ralph warns him, 'When you see me coming down the street, get on the other side.'

Ed replies, 'When you come down the street, there ain't no other side.'

In the same episode, when Ralph declines dinner with the Nortons, he says, 'It won't hurt me to wait a couple of hours to eat.'

Ed counters, 'No, it won't hurt you, but it'll be tough on the farmers.'

When Norton discovers that Alice's pet name for Ralph when they were first courting was her 'little buttercup', he says, 'You were a cup of butter and now you're a whole tub of lard.'

In 'A Matter of Life and Death,' Ralph considers selling his body to science so that he will have money to leave to Alice. Norton quips, 'If they pay by the pound, Alice'll be a millionaire.'

Alice gets in her share of digs. In 'Mind Your Own Business,' Ralph vows that he is going down to the sewer to get Norton's job back. He

*Above:* **Twenty-five years later, Norton and Ralph still bowled on lane number three.**

*Opposite page:* **The cast of the new *Honeymooners*: husbands Ralph Kramden and Ed Norton were still portrayed by Jackie Gleason and Art Carney. The wives, Alice Kramden and Trixie Norton, however, were played by Sheila McCrae and Jane Kean, respectively.**

says, 'There's nothing in this world gonna stop me from going down to the sewer tomorrow morning.'

Alice counters, 'Oh no? There isn't a manhole in New York you could fit through.'

Alice doesn't share Ralph's and Norton's optimism when it comes to their future of fame and fortune. When Ralph is hoping to be discovered by a talent scout, he cites Kirk Douglas, who was a soda jerk before Hollywood found him. To Ralph, this means that he himself might be discovered. To Alice, it means that there is an opening for a soda jerk.

Like honeymooners, Alice and Ralph have no children. When Ralph finds a baby on the bus, he and Alice could never have kept the child, though millions of Americans were rooting for the adoption to go through. Ralph is not ready for fatherhood. He is too much of a child himself. Alice can take care of herself, but people would have felt sorry for the baby. As **Honeymooners** writer Walter Stone said, even Lucy Ricardo didn't really keep her baby. 'Once the comic material was exhausted, you didn't see much of Little Ricky. He would have gotten in the way of the plots.' Besides, there were plenty of shows in the 1950s that were busily exploring every possible plot twist in bringing up baby.

Most fans would probably agree, however, that the best **Honey-mooners** episode is the one in which Ralph Kramden finds an abandoned baby on his bus and brings it home. In their excitement, Alice and Ralph try to fix up their dismal apartment so that they can adopt the baby. The audience laughed and cried so much that they couldn't fit the performance into a half-hour time slot. They had to continue the story the following week. When the baby's mother showed up to claim her, Americans grieved.

Male supremacy is one of Ralph's most dearly held tenets. When he loses his job, Alice offers to go to work. Ralph won't hear of it. He says he'd rather see her starve, that they'll just have to live on their savings. Alice replies, 'That'll carry us through the night, but what'll we do in the morning?'

Ralph's expostulations on marriage do not jibe with what actually occurs at 328 Chauncey. In the episode titled 'Here Comes the Bride,' Ralph tells his future brother-in-law, Stanley, 'You are the king, because a man's home is his castle, and in that castle you're the king… Tomorrow afternoon when Agnes says "I do," that is the last decision you allow her to make.' In another episode, the would-be marriage counselor instructs a friend, 'Every time you get into the habit of saying yes to your wife, you're getting into the habit of saying no to your independence.'

But Ralph shows his true colors in the episode entitled 'T'was the Night Before Christmas' when he says, 'Boy, what a pleasure it is to think that you've got someplace to go to. And the place that you're going to, there's somebody in it that you really love. Somebody you're nuts about.'

## The Schemes

Ralph makes $62 a week as a bus driver (Norton makes the same in the sewer.) He can't help but dream of the big day when he will be a rich man. Not only does Ralph dream, but he and his sidekick make every effort to make these dreams come true. In one of the early skits, Ralph and Ed see a building going up and decide to erect a hotdog stand across the street. They are going to sell hotdogs to the lunch-time crowd and make millions. 'Would you believe only yesterday I was driving a bus?' Ralph crows, only to find out that the building going up is a Howard Johnson's.

Another time, Ralph and Norton buy the land across the street from the new movie house that is under construction, and decide to turn it into a parking lot. Once again, they think they have a sure thing, until they discover that the movie theatre is a drive-in.

*Previous pages:* **Trixie (Jane Kean) almost makes the gang (Art Carney, Sheila McCrae, and Jackie Gleason) miss the gang plank as they head off for Europe. Forty-two episodes were set in Europe, but these episodes have never been rerun since their original airing.**

*Above:* **The Nortons' and the Kramdens' cruise to Europe is filled with comic disasters, beginning with a fire in their cabin.**

*Opposite page:* **Norton and Ralph raise their glasses to the lads and lasses in a Irish pub.**

Some of Ralph and Ed's other schemes—all with similar results—were glow-in-the-dark wallpaper, to save on electricity; a uranium field in Asbury Park; KramMar Mystery Appetizer—which turned out to be dog food—and no-cal pizza. But no matter what happens to Ralph and Norton, they always end up no better and no worse than they were before. When Ralph mails an insulting letter to his boss, he regains his job by episode's end. When he wins a trip to Europe, he is the same bumbling fool in every country he visits, and he returns to the same humble 'castle' in Bensonhurst. The successful formula for the show relies upon predictable situations and defined characters.

## Raccoon Lodge

During the live broadcasts, names of characters and institutions often changed. The Raccoon lodge was called by two different names, depending upon the episode: The International Order of Friendly Raccoons and The Royal Order of Raccoons. The uniform is an usher's suit and a Davy Crockett coonskin cap. The Grand High Exalted Mystic Ruler's hat has three tails hanging off it, and the Raccoon of the Year is allowed a platinum braid instead of gold. The entrance requirements for the hopeful Raccoon candidate are: he must have a public school diploma, have been a resident of the United States for the last six

months, and pay a $1.50 initiation fee. The Raccoon handshake involves touching elbows and bouncing the Raccoon tails. The Raccoon song goes like this:

### RACCOON ALMA MATER
From the hallowed streets of Greenpoint*,
To the shores of Sheepshead Bay,
From the Verrazano Narrows,
To Carnarsie across the way...
We have come together, one and all,
In fellowship to commune,
And to glorify the Grand Exalted
Brotherhood of Raccoons.

*pronounced *Greenpernt*

The Raccoon of the Year gets to wear a platinum braid on his uniform. He can run for Grand High Exalted Mystic Ruler. He opens the first clam at the annual clambake, steers from the bridge on the Raccoon boat ride up the Hudson River as they pass Raccoon Point, and he and his wife get free burial in the Raccoon National Cemetery in Bismarck, North Dakota.

# IT'S A WRAP

**A**fter 39 episodes, and with at least 39 more owed to Buick, Gleason called an end to the Chauncey Street saga. The people who had arranged his contract with Buick were shocked. **Honeymooners** fans were shocked. Gleason simply shrugged and said, 'The excellence of the material could not be maintained, and I have too much fondness for the show to cheapen it.'

The last episode aired 22 September 1956, in which Ralph tries to impress an old friend by pretending to run the bus company instead of being merely a driver.

Ownership of the 39 episodes reverted back to Jackie after three years, but he turned around and sold them outright to CBS, and later rued the day that he gave up the goose who laid the golden egg. Art Carney and Joyce Randolph received residuals for a while, but only Audrey Meadows continues to receive them. Her manager fought for her residuals long before anyone took such things seriously. The whole idea of reruns was new enough that few people realized the potential gold mine in syndication.

The week following the last show, Jackie returned to live television with **The Jackie Gleason Show**. The Kramdens and Nortons continued to bicker and bowl, now sponsored by Bulova watches and Old Gold cigarettes. The pressure was off to produce a half hour of wonderful comedy twice a week. When Jackie felt the material justified it, Ralph, Alice, Ed and Trixie would sometimes get the entire hour to themselves. Some weeks, they didn't appear at all.

There have been several Trixies in the 28-year span of **Honeymooners** production, and even several Alices, but there's been only one Norton. If Art Carney wasn't available, the Honeymooners did not go on. Art Carney left the show after the 1956-57 season in order to devote more time to his acting, and Buddy Hackett joined the cast. That season was to be the last to feature **The Honeymooners** until 1962.

Then Jackie captained a game show called **You're in the Picture** (1961) which was so terrible that he himself cancelled it after the first week. The second week, he came out and apologized to the audience, then spent the rest of the season conducting a celebrity talk show in that same time slot. Later, he introduced his successful variety show, **Jackie Gleason and His American Scene Magazine** (1962-1966), which consisted of celebrities and skits. There was a brief attempt—from

*Opposite page:* **Known the world over as 'the Great One' and 'Mr Saturday Night,' Jackie Gleason was known to his friends as a good-hearted Brooklyn wisenheimer.**

*Left:* Is it Norton...? Not really. This drawing, a CBS press release for *The Jackie Gleason Show: The American Scene Magazine*, depicts Reginald Van Gleason III and his 'special caddies... Gleason Girls Darlene Enlow (blonde) and Greta Randall (brunette).' While it may look like Norton driving the cart, it's actually comedian Frank Fontaine. At the time, the autumn of 1964, Art Carney was pursuing other acting challenges, and true to his promise, Gleason never used any other actor to play Norton.

*Right:* When Carney was ready to reprise his old role as Norton, Gleason brought back *The Honeymooners* and took the show—in fiction though not in fact—to Europe. Here, the boys show off their cruise wear.

29 September to 27 October 1962—to recreate **The Honeymooners**, with Sue Ann Langdon as Alice, and Patricia Wilson as Trixie, whenever Art Carney was available to appear as Norton.

At that time, the reruns of the original 39 were being shown in such places as Australia, Surinam, Iran, Nigeria and Saudi Arabia. However, at home in 1965, Gleason's current show was losing the ratings war to such unlikely competitors as **Flipper** and **I Dream of Jeannie**. He even announced his retirement. Suddenly, though, he became re-inspired. He signed an $8 million contract with CBS for one more season. He vowed at a press conference that the new program would be different, better. He admitted that some of his recent shows 'looked like they had been made on the way to the men's room.'

Jackie had always complained about the New York City winters, and finally, in 1966, the entire cast and crew, dancers, the press and a Dixieland band boarded a train bound for Miami. When asked in an interview if there was a bar on the train, Gleason replied, 'Are you kidding? The whole train was a bar.' The 10-day public relations blowout party was such a success that '**The Great Gleason Express**' was repeated in 1964 and 1965. Jackie was signed up for 32 shows, 10 of which were to be new musical **Honeymooners** episodes.

Left, above: Norton and Ralph put on the Ritz at a Parisian café.

Left: Their African safari almost ends in disaster when Norton is monkeying around.

Above: Trixie (Jane Kean), Alice (Sheila McCrae), Norton (Art Carney) and Ralph (Jackie Gleason) visit Buckingham Palace to see the changing of the guard.

## A Second Honeymoon

Years before, when the old **Honeymooners** show had ended, Gleason had ordered that the set be struck. Knowing his boss's mercurial temperament, chief set decorator Phil Cuoco had secretly preserved the old set, down to the drip pan. When the cast debarked the '**Great Gleason Express**' in Miami, they found the same props, furniture—even the same windows and walls.

Many of the new episodes were reconstructed from the earliest **Honeymooners** episodes—the ones that were never taped from the DuMont network. There were some differences between the old and the new, however. The new shows were in color and were a full hour long. There was a new Alice and a new Trixie, and the whole cast periodically burst into song. Unlike the 1950s shows, they weren't filmed in New York (and certainly not in Europe,) but in Miami. Sheila McCrae portrayed Alice, with Jane Kean as Trixie. Art Carney had been busy creating the roles of the Archer on **Batman** and Felix Unger in **The Odd Couple** on Broadway, but returned to play Ed Norton, sewer worker.

The new **Honeymooners** were so well-liked that the 10 episodes originally planned grew to 42. The Nortons and the Kramdens travelled to Africa, Italy, Ireland, Spain, France, Germany and England before returning to 328 Chauncey Street for Christmas.

**Left:** Jackie Gleason cohosted *The Mike Douglas Show* for a week in January of 1976. Broadcast from oceanside and poolside in Miami Beach, the guests included Sean Connery, Michael Caine, Larry Csonka and Milton Berle.

**Above:** A thin Jackie Gleason joined Julie Andrews for a joint television special entitled, *How Sweet It Is*.

**Right:** Julie played Norton on *How Sweet It Is*. Jackie had been true to his promise: an actress, never another *actor*, portrayed Norton.

**Above, right:** Jackie lost some weight before this Bing Crosby Christmas special, but the Great One could still cut a Santa-like figure with Katherine Crosby.

Above: Ralph is 'just reading the articles' in this 1978 *Honeymooners* special.

*Opposite page, above:* Audrey Meadows came out of her show business retirement to join Jackie Gleason and Templeton Fox in *The Honeymooners—The Second Honeymoon*, in which Alice and Ralph celebrate their twenty-fifth wedding anniversary. The special aired 2 February 1976, after Gleason had moved to ABC.

*Opposite page, below:* How sweet is it? Judging by the expressions on their faces, the grapes are a little sour as Trixie (Jane Kean), Ed Norton (Art Carney, of course), Ralph (Jackie Gleason) and Alice (Audrey Meadows) celebrate with a bottle of wine on the 1976 *Honeymooners* special.

Then the original Alice Gibson Kramden reappeared on the show, this time as Mrs. Gibson, Alice's mother. Jackie had for once delegated some of the casting responsibilities, and was surprised to find Pert Kelton back on the show. He found it a bit insensitive to ask a woman 'of a certain age' to play the mother of a character she herself had played 15 years before. On 4 March 1967, however, there she was, insulting Ralph left and right, just like old times.

Gleason had been doing **The Honeymooners** as just a portion of his variety show. One week, the entire hour might be allotted for the Kramdens and the Nortons; another week, they might not appear at all. In 1970, CBS decided that they wanted one hour a week of **The Honeymooners** alone. Gleason didn't want to do that. Despite a regular seat in the top fifteen, if not the top ten, Nielsen rated shows, Jackie went off the air.

The network was also courting a younger audience. Gleason's audience at the time tended to be long-time fans who had co-opted 'The Great One' as their very own. The younger generation, whom advertisers began to discover in the mid-1960s, were not watching **The Jackie Gleason Show**. 'They couldn't find anything to sell to the people who were watching,' Jackie said. 'They seemed to think that people who

*These pages:* **Scenes from the Christmas special of 1977.** *Above:* **An exchange of gifts.** *Opposite page:* **In the Christmas show down at the Gotham Bus Company, Ralph plays Bob Cratchitt to Norton's Tiny Tim.**

watched us didn't buy anything.' Gleason and the network's mutual break-up made way for **All in the Family** in the slot of Saturday night, leading some to remark that Ralph Kramden and Archie Bunker had never been seen in a room together. There was speculation that the two never shared a screen for the same reason as Clark Kent and Superman.

Gleason did not renew his 15-year work-or-no-work $100,000 contract with CBS when it ran out in 1972. He chose instead to sign with NBC for a year, and when that didn't work out, he switched to ABC where he put together three **Honeymooners** specials, each an hour long. Ralph and Alice celebrated their 25th wedding anniversary on 2 February 1976, and on 28 November 1977, Jackie, Audrey and Art were reunited for a Christmas special. In the resurrected program, Ralph is in charge of the Christmas show down at the bus garage. He puts on a production of **A Christmas Carol**. In a bit of a role reversal, Ralph plays Daddy (Bob) Cratchitt to Norton's Scrooge *and* Tiny Tim. Jane Kean plays Trixie playing Tiny Tim's sister.

Just prior to the Valentine's Day special (13 February 1978), which, as usual, was shot without retakes before a live audience, everyone came down with the flu. Rehearsals were delayed when Art Carney got sick

enough to have to go to the hospital. Meanwhile, the writers and actors kept changing the script. As he lifted a heavy medical dictionary in rehearsal, Jackie ad-libbed, 'I hope it has some information about hernias.' The line was cut an hour before curtain.

Finally, an hour before show time on Friday, executive producer Jack Philbin asked, 'Do you think we're overrehearsed?' Art Carney groaned, 'Maybe I was better off in the hospital.'

*Honeymooners* segments from the early Gleason hour-long variety shows finally saw the blue light of reruns in 1986 on ShowTime Cable Television. Because the episodes are not neat half-hour segments, they had not been shown since their original airing. The cable station put together a special amalgamation supplemented by interviews with the cast. *The Honeymooners* continues to find new audiences with the younger generations.

To maintain popularity for so many years, there must be more than simply good writing and a wonderful cast. In Gleason's vision, there is an element of truth with which the audience identifies. Even if they've never been to Brooklyn, people watching the show knew that what Ralph was doing this week was true to the character he had shown the week before.

*Above:* Jackie played the wicked conman Gondorff in *The Sting II.*

*Left:* Art Carney and Jackie Gleason starred together in a television movie called *Izzy and Moe,* based on a true story about a pair of Prohibition-era policemen.

*At right:* Jackie played Sheriff Buford T Justice — the 'Smokey' of the title — in the Burt Reynold's 1977 movie, *Smokey and the Bandit.* Smokey is a CB code word for highway patrolman.

# ONE OF THESE DAYS

**D**uring its long run, **The Honeymooners** was extremely influential on other programs. The show practically created the sitcom as we know it today. Many of the story-lines which have been done on other shows a hundred times were original creations by the writing staff of **The Honeymooners**. **The Flintstones** is one of the more obvious examples of a **Honeymooners**-inspired production: a stone age version of **The Honeymooners**, with Fred as Ralph, the red-haired Wilma as Alice, next-door sidekick Barney Rubble as Norton (with Mel Blanc doing Barney's voice) and Betty as Trixie, Barney's wife and Wilma's best friend.

Norman Lear also loved to take old **Honeymooner's** plots and adopt them for Archie Bunker on **All in the Family**, the show which took the place of the Gleason show after its cancellation. Rarely had television chosen the working class for portrayal in its sitcoms, finding little humor in poverty and grim surroundings. Ralph Kramden and Archie Bunker both face the company physical with dread; Alice Kramden and Edith Bunker both get jobs against Ralph's and Archie's wishes; Ralph and Archie both have reunions with a successful friend. Lear's version of these events was typically darker than Gleason's.

There is also **The Honeymooners/Odd Couple** connection. Art Carney created the character of Felix Unger on Broadway, and maintained close friendships with people involved with the Neil Simon play. When the play was made into a movie and then brought to television, it bore some traces of **The Honeymooners**: Alice worked at Krausmeyer's Bakery; years later, on **The Odd Couple**, Oscar Madison uses Krausmeyer's Bakery as his campaign headquarters.

Ralph's jealousy and Alice's secretiveness may keep the Nortons and Kramdens from a peaceful existence. Norton and Ralph's schemes may never make them rich. Ralph may never be Raccoon of the Year (although Norton is), but Ralph continues to scheme, and to hope. He still has his wife, his best friend and his dreams. He never complains, he never gives up.

**Opposite page: The happy couple celebrates 25 years of being everyone's favorite honeymooners.**

# INDEX